Different Worlds

Konah B.

Different Worlds
© 2024, Rebekah Patterson
ISBN: 978-1-966337-00-3

First Edition, 2024

Printed in the United States of America

Edited by Cherice Cameron
Cover Design by Aysia Turner
Layout Design by Erica Castro

To my Younger self, may you finally find peace from your past.

Table of Contents

Preface

At Simply Youth Institute (SYI), we believe that leadership starts with understanding oneself and the world around us. Through programs like SAGACITY, we empower young people to share their truths, embrace their identities, and use their voices to inspire change. Konah Bryant's memoir, *Different Worlds*, profoundly reflects this mission—it is a deeply personal story about navigating the complexities of identity, belonging, and resilience in a culture that often feels adversarial.

Arriving in America as a six-year-old, Konah faced numerous challenges that tested her sense of self. She dealt with the heavy burdens of cultural displacement, trauma, and the expectations of a new society. However, her journey extended beyond mere survival. *Different Worlds* delves into themes of identity that encompass much more than her experience as an immigrant: it explores the tension between faith and self-discovery, the intersection of culture and sexuality, and the courage needed to reconcile the many facets of her identity in a world that often prefers simplicity.

Through her raw honesty, Konah reveals the profound search for home—both physically and within herself. Her narrative examines the religious ideals that shaped her upbringing while finding the freedom to question, redefine, and ultimately embrace a more authentic version of herself. It is a journey of confronting shame, reclaiming agency, and building a foundation of pride and leadership.

At SYI, Konah's story serves as inspiration for participants in the SAGACITY program and beyond. Her ability to transform personal struggles into platforms for advocacy is a testament to her resilience and determination. *Different Worlds* embodies the idea that leadership can emerge from unexpected places—through self-reflection, vulnerability, and the courage to embrace one's full identity.

This memoir is not just a story of survival; it is one of transformation. It challenges readers to think critically about the systems, beliefs, and biases that shape our lives and to consider what it means to live authentically in a world that often resists change.

Konah Bryant's story is a gift, inviting readers to explore their own journeys through her courage and wisdom. *Different Worlds* is more than a book; it is a call to recognize the beauty in identity's complexity and to create space for others to do the same.

Welcome to Konah's world. May her journey inspire you to navigate your own with boldness, compassion, and an unwavering sense of self.

The Orphanage

Dear Younger Self,

    I have watched you grow up. I've been with you since the beginning of time when your younger self sacrificed your innocence with the betrayal of leaving home. See, home has never been a destination for you, it's been about love. You have always needed unconditional love to know that you are enough. Your younger self deserved so much more. That was not the case, love didn't come naturally to you. Your younger self taught herself how to learn how to survive without the support or presence of a mother or father. Your battles were yours alone and yours to fight alone without any protection. See, younger self, your story began long before you were aware of it. You have been your story all along.

Dear Younger Self,

You were brought into this world whereas a six year old little girl, you have experienced more hardships and have endured more pain than people could think of, but you never gave up. Your younger self has experienced more loneliness, rejection, abandonment, and betrayal than most at the age of six. It has been one hell of a storm.

Different Worlds

Dear Younger Self,
As I am writing this, the first time I saw you I remember the six year old little girl who always managed to find her own sunshine regardless of where your life was at even if you didn't understand it. You have been beautiful to watch, six years old you always carry so much love, kindness, gentleness and compassion with you. Kindness and compassion has always lived inside you as though it's been your home. The first time I saw you dear black girl, I saw a reflection that you remain smart and kind. You never needed protection because you have been your own warrior. You stepped into a whole new world, finding yourself confused and disconnected from the world where the things in your life turned you into a fighter, strengthening your fall because the harder you seem to fall the higher you have bounced.

Dear Younger Self,
You have always been enough. You were never told by your mommy and daddy how loved you are. You missed out on goodnight kisses

and daddy calling you his little girl. From the day I saw you, you have always been your own spitfire. You may have been seen as different but you never got to hear those words from either your mommy or daddy telling you that you are beautiful and that your uniqueness is beautiful. Your life was taken away from you far from stolen without you having a say in it.

Dear Black Girl,
You were not involved in the process of your life when your mamma decided the best thing for you and your sister was to give you up, hoping for a better life. Your life completely changed without ever knowing where home was. See, dear black girl, you weren't asked whether or not you wanted to be taken away from your momma. Every decision making involved in your adoption was out of your control. The older version of you (Konah) is asking why would I ever want to leave the only place that has been my home. Younger me cries out and says I never want to leave you mamma because I love you. Your daddy was never in the picture so you missed out on hearing your daddy call you his little princess.

Dear Younger Self,
You became your own little hero even if daddy was never home for you. Six year old version of you missed the chance to say I love you. The older version of me now looks back and says I never got a chance to tell you I love you daddy. Little girl was long in the storm before she was even aware of her magic.

Dear Black Girl,
You were cheated out in your adolescent years and everything that makes up who you are as you are about to enter into a world that you do not understand.

Dear Younger Konah,
I've been watching over you since you were six years old. You were never alone nor are you walking alone. I've always been with you.

You were too young to understand why daddy left you behind and wasn't around much. You were a little girl not knowing any better what was going to come of your life when you and your sister turned six.

Dear Younger Self,
Why were two six year old girls already experiencing so much loss and pain in such little time. Daddy, I never got to say I love you and goodbye. Never learned your face, never had a chance to hear your voice, to hold your hand, to play tag or hide-seek with you. You have always been a daddy's girl but you never got the chance to spend time with me.

Dear Younger Self,
I can only imagine the deep wound of watching you grow up without your daddy ever holding you, taking a nap with you or even getting to sit on your lap and talk with you. See, younger self never you lost the experience of what it's like to have a mommy and daddy to love you. When I needed you the most you weren't there without any goodbyes or me getting to wave my little hands to you.

Dear Younger Self,
Your war in your mind started the day when your daddy wasn't around to let you know how important you are. Your life flashed before your eyes. Dear younger self, it's time that your story is written and heard. You have always been protected from the time of your arrival at the orphanage. I watched you walk into that village with your hands being held by strangers and unfamiliar faces as you and your sister make an entrance into a strange place.

Dear Younger Self,
You have learned not to be a stranger to the dark. You have been in the dark and have experienced the dark. You have learned to not only live but be resilient with all the scars and pain that your little heart went through. You have learned to stand strong be

cause there's always been a place for you. As you and your sister come into this village with strangers, you walk in silence as you are brought into an unfamiliar place. As you enter this new environment, you are walking on a dirt road where pebbles are spread out big and small. The large building you're walking up to is a shade of light and dark blue combined.

To get inside the building of the orphanage we had to go up five stairs. The roof on the orphanage had an overhang that helped keep rain out. The set up as we entered the orphanage was a one story balcony made up of cement. We were two sisters walking in the daylight to a new place soon to be a new home. The sun was shining bright but filled with humidity.

It was a beautiful day when my sister and I heard other kids our age and older laughing, running around and chasing one another, and saw mothers sitting under a tree feeding their babies and socializing. As we walked into the village, we were looked at with curiosity. Having my hands held brought me safety and comfort. My little hands felt clammy and sweaty as I was looking around the place with an open mind and my mind was full of wonders of what this new life was going to bring. As we toured the inside of the orphanage, there is a crowd of people who look like us scattered in various directions, mainly mothers. Not many fathers were present. Holding onto a stranger's hand and to my sister made me less scared. I didn't want to let go of my sister's hand or the strangers that were with us throughout this transition in our life. The hands of my sister's and these strangers were so soft and gentle. I wasn't ready for them to leave our side. When we entered the inside of the building the air was cold, the ground was just cement. The inside of the building smelled of mold, rust, human flesh, urine and sweat. There was no decoration of any kind inside of the orphanage which was rather dull.

The orphanage did not feel welcoming to me as I looked around with curiosity. It was dusty looking. Our new home didn't feel like home. We were in the care of strangers. The building was empty. There was no furniture; chairs, tables, benches or even beds. Food and water weren't easily accessible. My sister and I came with our own bag of clothing and shoes. There were no windows to look through and the orphanage was also dark as we continued to tour. There wasn't much to tour because it was just one big building crowded with unfamiliar faces.

As we continued to explore the orphanage, down the hall were three different rooms. On the right side of the hall were two smaller bedrooms. The first room could hold an estimated ten people. The last room, down the hall to the right, was where my sister and I were placed. It had a bed big enough for two but it was for a man and a woman, not for us.. My sister and I were once again placed with strangers and we only had the concrete and cement floor to rest on. The room on the far left corner, across from where my sister and I resided, was massive. This room was also dull, not only dark and filthy. The moisture in the air was damp and cold, lingering. This larger room had enough sleeping space for a crowd of hundred people sleeping in columns of three. In this room there were mats, many mats, lying across the floor all squished together. These woven mats spread from one end of the room to the other. Lots and lots of mothers were present with young ones. Very few fathers were present. With limited space to move around mothers and children huddled together at night to stay warm.

Seeing other children our age with their mommies and some fathers brought me confusion as to why our mommy and daddy weren't with us.
After touring the orphanage the strangers that were with us left. Now we were all alone but that didn't stop us from being kids. Very shy at first, we hung around each other daily. We never went some-place without each other. We were all each other had in the world. It took us a few days to warm up to our new home. A few days before we started running off and playing with other children. Our life changed so drastically that all of the transitions that trans-pired throughout our adoption process were lost to me. As two six year old girls, one can only imagine the burdens we were carrying around even if we were too young to comprehend what was hap-pening. There was no time to fully process anything that was going on around us. This limited our stress response and reaction. Run-

process but cincumstances didn't lead to that. The only comfort and security we had were each other. We were numb. Our first night together, alone in the orphanage, without the presence of our daddy and mommy was the most confusing. I laid awake with my six year old mind in chaos.

That night, we went to bed in the oppressively damp, cold, and hard room. We had no mommy or daddy to care for us. No mommy or daddy to tell us goodnight my princess's. No mommy or daddy to give us goodnight kisses. No mommy or daddy to hold us at night. No mommy or daddy to hug. No mommy or daddy around to put us to sleep. No mommy or daddy to tell us that we are going to be okay. No mommy or daddy to tell us that we deserve more in life. No mommy or daddy to tell us that we are smart. No mommy or daddy to run to when in need of safety. No mommy or daddy to tell us that we are enough. No mommy or daddy to cry out to when we got scared. No mommy or daddy to cuddle with to help us fall asleep.

In the orphanage, strangers had to learn to live together. The living spaces were forced. People on both the left and right of each other had their skin compressed in tight spaces provided to them. At night, there were crying mothers, babies and children.

Chaos and Poverty

The orphanage was dark and gloomy, dimly lit. The only source of light we had were lanterns. Even then, that wasn't enough to sustain stability and security. Realizing my six year old brain knewg that mommy or daddy weren't going to be with us made the nights, days, weeks, and months long without them. Night time, falling asleep, was avoided at all costs. Sleeping became increasingly unmanageable. Once the lanterns went out, there was nothing to replace the light with.

Obtaining items needed for living comfortably was difficult. There were very few people with finances or the chance and opportunity to purchase oil in the market. Children without their parents' existence to help out, like me and my sister, went without. We were two little girls left in a strange place, laying on a concrete floor on thin mats no bigger than a towel, in darkness and cold. The mats were woven by hand, from bamboo strips, a dark shade of brown. Lying on these mats brought discomfort at night. I could felt the hardness of the floor press sharply down my spine, hurting my six year old body. The more tossing that happened, the more my bones were grinding against the mats and floor, bruising my body. We both cuddled close to each other to keep warm. Some nights it was even harder to sleep because of the cold.

Darkness was frightening and I would experience sudden wake ups in the middle of the night and a fear of needing to go to the bathroom. Waking up meant facing the dark, not just the dark in our room, but the dark that led to the underground hole where waste was disposed. The nicest term for this is " restroom." We used leaves to wipe with, or nothing at all. Most often, in the blackness of night I was too terrified to open my eyes.

If my sister was awake, we would be brave the night trek together. The thought of walking alone made it necessary for me to keep my eyes shut and wait till the nightmare was over, ignoring my bladder. Being so fearful of the dark would often result in wetting the bed. The dark made our sleeping arrangements on the ground, bugs crawling on us, horrific. As an adult now, just the thought of centipedes, pill bugs, earwigs, and beetles makes my skin crawl. Then insects were a punishment win themselves. Eventually fear of being beaten with a tree branch forced me to face my demons and my fear of the dark ended.

The only time I ever was able to find rest was when my sister and I would bundle up close, keeping the other warm, especially on nights it rained. When it rained the sound was music to my ears. Rain brought me joy, peace, security, and comfort. The loud sound made beautiful music as raindrops fell on the tin roof of the orphanage. Going to sleep with the rain falling still sends goosebumps rising through my arms and back. Rain hitting the tin roof was therapeutic to me. Somehow the sound made me feel safe, I could relax my mind and body.

When morning came, the night sky would become bright orange with the sweet smell of lukewarm air. The sounds of other children brought my heart happiness. Hearing constant laughter and loud noises coming from different locations put my mind at ease and filled me with peace. Hearing other children play, laugh, and having my sister by my side helped maintain my sanity. Joy was short-lived in the orphanage and strangers, filth, bugs, darkness, and sleepless nights, were not the most daunting things we faced.

Hunger. Hunger was the real challenge. Without parents,

my sister and I had to fend for ourselves. You can imagine how hard it was for two little girls to provide their own food. Not knowing any better, we resorted to eating dirt from the ground. We were too young to understand how abnormal it was to shovel handfuls of dirt into our mouths. All we understood is that the dirt helped lessen the pain in our bellies. We understood that we needed to stay alive. We lacked the understanding of what was normal and what wasn't at the time. Eating dirt was the harsh reality of two girls with very little support.

Dear Younger Self,
You did what you needed to sustain from hunger and did what was necessary to stay alive. Looking back now, the best parts of your younger years were cherished when it came to eating your favorite foods which brought you happiness and filled up your little belly.

Later in life I missed the taste of fried sardines in my mouth as I adapted to the American way of living. I wonder now who would ever have considered the thought of eating insects to be delicious ? Better than insects, eating rice mixed in with sardines was peace to my stomach. I find it hard to believe my own stories of survival, even as I reflect. As I write and ask myself how it is I could have been okay with my willingness to eat insects and dirt. The simple answer is that I learned to appreciate the little food we could find. We had to stay in survival mode. When my litle tummy was hungry there was very little time to complain about the things that you didn't. The only thing a parent desires is that their kids are safe and know they have a home to come back to. This wasn't the case with us, two six-year-old orphans.

Eventually we knew that there was no home to go back to. Our little tummies were constantly hungry. We had no mommy or daddy to rely on to provide for us. Deep frying grasshoppers, crickets, termites, and snails, and killing large snakes were the only available food sources we had, even if it meant dealing with upset stomachs because of parasites. Fried plantains were part of our everyday diet. In fact, lots of fruits were eaten; such as plums (known as mangos here in America), bananas, and coconut.

Dear Younger Self,

Being the rambunctious little girl so full of spirit, kept you dreaming and reaching for the stars. Your days of climbing many banana, coconut, and plum trees made your mind an adventurous and curious creature.
Even back then, you had your own independence exploring the world around you whenever opportunities called for your younger self to be you, you were seeking out freedom which kept you most alive throughout those daily struggles of life even if you lacked the understanding back then. You may have felt lost, confused and unseen, but your unconscious knows you weren't alone. Your innocence and happiness was stolen from you when you were so young but you still always managed to give everyone a part of your heart.

Dear Younger Self,
Someone has been with you through every storm in your life, giving you what you have needed every step of the way and has been by your side , your family and loved ones. The moments where you were most scared and felt lonely, the universe lived inside you when you subconsciously did not know how to carry on. The things that kept your six year old wild heart and mind alive were your days of having independence.

Dear Younger Self,
You were just a little girl protecting herself from the danger of guns and very little money while watching over your sister as well, making sure you two always stuck together.

We had very little understanding of what sources we needed to stay in that constant survival mode . Scrounging for food from day to day became a very normal routine for us throughout this time. We had limited options without parents around to help meet our needs so growing up had to happen quickly. Learning how to cook and provide for ourselves was needed. Cooking dry rice mixed in with savory and creamy sardines was the most delicious thing I enjoyed binging on.

Dear Younger Self,
Lack of human resources and inadequate funding for basic necessities made living very difficult, but you learned how to manage and care for yourself. The surrounding of our community made it impossible to never lose hope that tomorrow will bring sunshine.

Dear Younger Self,
The sight of seeing friendly faces kept hope alive even if it seemed unbearable. You had no choice but to learn how to find joy in the little things. Without structure or parental guidance freedom was easily accessible to all kids growing up as orphans. Even more, the poverty level of growing up in Liberia made access to school less of a priority, affecting many children to receive quality of education.

Attendance with school was not consistent. The times that I found my self in the classroom allowed me to learn my ABC'S and counting. The school was down the road from the orphanage and my sister and I either went to school together or went with other kids around our age, wearing blue and white uniforms.

Dear Younger Self,
Days that you weren't in school, you and your sister spent a lot of your time exploring and traveling long distances by foot. You had no concept of what transportation was so your little feet traveled on dirt paths and roads.

Living as orphans, a majority of children like me learned to adapt to an environment surrounded by guns. Without guidance, it became a natural part of our daily existence to protect each other by sticking together. One weekday in the life of orphans was delegated to Sunday school attendance and children, mothers, and fathers dressed their Sunday best.

Seeing the gathering of those who attended church always lifted my spirits up, especially when it came to singing and joining other kids in Sunday school. If the sun was out, so was I. Although freedom kept my sanity alive we found it hard to escape from the poverty in which we were living. One of the chores assigned to us in the orphanage included taking baths in plastic buckets. Navigating drawing water from a well included attaching a rope to a bucket handle and gently lowering the bucket down the well. Depending on the size of bucket we bathed in we could either stand up or sit down but most of the time we stood up. These traditional ways of bathing did not prevent us from maintaining good hygiene.
In a similar fashion, wash rags and bar soap did the job to keep us clean. The washing of clothes was done with wooden washing boards. The washing boards varied in sizes from small, medium, and large, each with a different use. Even being so little if we could get our hands dirty, our little bodies held and used the small washing boards. We stood behind the washboards as our bodies ground clothes against the boards. Being the high spirited little girl I was hardship never stopped me from being independent. In spite of the living conditions I somehow managed to find something to hold onto that kept my heart cheerful. By the same token, learning to keep up with hygiene entailed finding small twigs from shrubs. We used these twigs to keep our teeth polished.

Dear Younger Self,
You are so free spirited, chasing the stars. Just like that, your world came falling down.

Living in the village had its advantages and disadvantages. For example, living in an area filled with wild monkeys instilled fear inside of me because they would attack. When my sister and I wanted to go out and explore different parts of the county we traveled by foot and often came across one or two wild monkeys. In order for us to get to a certain location traveling on dirt roads, we sometimes had to cross over gutter creeks. Once as we traveled, we spotted one wild monkey standing in the middle of the dirt road. Because of the problem with the monkeys we would hesitate to pass through the road and would have to stay closer to the country. We weren't always prepared to face the wild monkeys.

We always managed to take the same route and eventually we made it a routine and became familiar with it. But we came prepared. We would make sure we did come ready to being in the presence of the wild monkeys. The monkeys were intimidating and it was scary to be in the presence of them. We had to remember to come armed. As a six-year-old girl who had a lot of energy, I had no fear of picking up a rock and throwing it at the monkeys in our presence. Africa had its moments of instilling fear inside of me. Fear of snakes was part of my daily nightmare. The size of these snakes made me really scared. Till this day, my fear of snakes is never ending. With my fear of snakes, the family-owned store that was within walking distance from the village wasn't the easiest to get to. To get to the store we had to walk down a narrow path. On both sides of this path were tall grasses and this is where the snakes hid. The snakes could be heard when they slithered around or hissed. Anytime I wanted to take the path that led to the local store, I had to find another route. I was frightened.

Sometimes I had to push through the fear to walk the path. I did. I would run so fast down the pathway so I wasn't attacked. I started challenging myself more and more to face my fears. Running through the pathway was the easiest and fastest way to get to the small shop. The other option of getting to the local owned store was to make a lap all the way around the landscape border. Going around took longer but I did what was necessary. The local store was where my sister and I spent most of our time socializing and visiting with neighbors and friends.

We would dance, sing, and listen to drums. I always enjoyed the laughter and smiles as other Africans would feast together out of a big bowl. The fire pit was located near the shop and it was here that cooking meals would occur. We had one meal a day to live off of but always managed. When we needed water to drink it would be fetched from the well and sometimes from a creek.

War Outbreak

Not only were the living conditions in the orphanage a nightmare, but the village where my sister and I resided was attacked. From a distance we could hear gunshots ranging and the sheer chaos of the moment happened unexpectedly. The sound of gunshots disturbed sleeping children, mothers, and fathers. There was little time to react whether that was trying to escape or trying to hide. The sound of screaming mothers and children's cries frightened me. I did not understand what was happening. We were so little and having time to react was not an option. We did not know how to respond to this drastic change in our environment, people scattered and ran but not all were successful.

As clueless and scared as we were, we somehow managed to escape from the bedroom where we were sleeping and found a hiding place inside the orphanage behind a door to avoid the chaos. The door we were hiding behind left just enough room for two little girls to hide. The spacing was confining and we stood there in silence. In fear. Holding tight onto one another's hands, we remained still not knowing when it was safe enough to come out from where we had hidden. Imagine the fear of two little girls alone in a strange place with so much happening and no time to respond. All we could hear from a distance was screaming and crying. We also witnessed people being killed, young people like me.

The inside of the orphanage was very dark. Being the size we were, we got away by staying hidden and leaving without being seen. Interestingly, we were hiding once again, but this time outside behind a group of tall bushes beyond the orphanage. Gunshots rang out again and the sheer chaos of the moment stained my memory. Some villagers managed to escape the gunfire and senseless violence. Others were not so lucky.

A strange man came from behind us, taking our hands and with him, we slowly made an exit out of the orphanage looking for an opportunity to escape. The stranger out of nowhere kept us safe from the violence. We would not have made it out alive without him. He hid and waited with us, as flashlights were pointed in the direction in the field of tall bushes. He did not leave our side till it was safe enough. There, in silence, my sister and I were restless, but my sister especially was shaken up from the sound of the guns. My sister began silently sobbing. At this moment, a risk because it meant us being exposed. The man who hid with us took his hand and covered her mouth to keep her from bursting out. In silence I sat with him and my sister. He held onto both of us. You can only imagine all the emotions welling up inside of two six year old girls hiding with a stranger.

Dear Younger Self,

I look back now and can see you being aware that something was not right. But a sense of peace was over you as a strange man kept you safe. You did not have much of an emotional response going on besides the feeling of being safe in the arms and caring of this older gentleman. You remained quiet and emotionally went numb. Having this man with you and your sister brought you a sense of comfort and security. For this reason, your fear lessened, and you stayed by his side till it felt safe to come out. You and your sister held each other's hands for comfort.

Those of us who made it out alive when the sound of guns was no longer heard were fortunate to have escaped. Without the help of the stranger my sister and I would not have made it out alive. It was not long before we were moved from the orphanage and were taken out of Bong County. We were put in the care of a woman we called Aunty, her daughter not much older than us, and a young man who was eighteen years of age. He was full grown and bigger than us. In this straw house Aunty had a bed with a comforter large enough for her and her little girl. Our sleeping arrangement was the same routine as the orphanage. My sister and I were placed on the hard concrete floor to sleep. We were not sleeping alone, but next to older gentlemen. Already fighting for survival in the unknown, our reality became more fraught. Now we were being sexually abused by the young man in the house nearly every night. There was no stopping him. My sister and I were prey for his own gratification. Night became his perfect opportunity to get what he wanted. Not knowing better, confused and small I was quiet as this man would pull my panties down and stick something inside me from behind.

Dear Younger Self,

You were two little girls with no mommy or daddy to protect you from this big and strong man. You were scared, just two little girls with nothing to defend yourselves with. You kept each other warm at night by huddling. No blanket to cover you from the cold, from the man. Again, you were one another's safety net. Nearly every night, I tried making an escape to Auntie's bed, hoping she would let me sleep with her and her daughter, but limited spacing kept me from getting away. I did not have much choice but to go lay down and cuddle with my sister. The man alternated his time between us. A lot of the nights I was in front of him, and he would touch me.

My little mind had a tough time comprehending what was happening to me at the time. All I knew then was that I did not have anywhere else to go. I felt alone and frightened without mommy or daddy around to call for help. Getting up to go to the restroom at night at this village didn't scare me as much as it did at the orphanage because I would squat not too far from the hut we were in. When my sister was left alone with the man, he would target her. When I came back, I would sleep behind my sister which meant being closer to the man every night. Months, days, and weeks passed without any protection. Sexual abuse became normal to us because there was no way out.

The duration of time it took waiting to be adopted was also the length of time this man had with us. Waiting for weeks, days, and months on end was suffering we paid with our bodies. The day finally arrived. It was a Sunday evening and my sister, and I were gathered together with four women. We were dressed in matching gowns and taken up to a house and left in confusion. We were taken from Auntie's where we had been residing with for about a year, and we were taken to the house of a woman where we celebrated and feasted. The feast was held in a light blue house and people took a photo of us in front of the house before we took off for America. My sister and I said our goodbyes after the dinner celebration, our last memory before leaving Africa for the next phase of our journey.

Children at Play

Dear Younger Self,

In spite of the hardship, I very much admire you and I am grateful that you and your sister were able to continue being kids. You had playtime with other children that consisted of slingshots, playing with dolls, building houses from sticks, and building toy cars using empty water bottles. You pierced the water bottles with a hot rod, making holes for the built in wheels. and you attached sticks to the empty water bottles. Strands of knot ropes or cotton ropes were also attached at the end near the lid. These things became your creative car.

Being the way I was, I spent my time as a little girl playing with slingshots, aiming at trees with rocks and pebbles, and aiming at and targeting trees. Building houses with sticks was one way that kept my mind and day busy. I also joined other children in the game of Double Dutch and found unused tire rims to play with. Running around pushing the tire rim was quite the workout for my little body, but I always had such a blast finding ways to release my energy. The African game of hopscotch not only was a game to be played, but it also taught educational matters when it came to learning numbers. Though it was fun, getting into the art and structure of numbers drawing and painting in each square kept me energized.

In the streets of Africa, children played in groups, getting to know each other and form friendships. Children played games of marbles. Games helped children grow and form healthy relationships. Marbles played in the streets kept kids alive by allowing them to be kids and pass time when struggle and poverty proved insufferable. Children spending time together encouraged fellowship and reinforced the fundamentals of socialization. It was not always easy getting access to marbles. If they were unavailable, children had to improvise using stones to continue playing the game. The game could be played with two or more players and by making a bigger circle with other children joined. More players made the game more exciting.

Marbles involved finding a location, digging a small hole in the dirt large enough for children to be able to move around the outside. Each player was given two marbles. One marble was placed on the ground, four spread-finger width away from the hole. The other marble was kept in one hand and used as a shooter. Each player took turns trying to hit the first marble into the hole. If a player was doing well in the game, he or she was given an A. Players scored a point when they hit the marble into the hole. Once the player hit their marble in the hole, they would try to hit another player's marble into the hole on their next turn. The more marbles a player hit into the hole, the higher their chance of becoming the overall winner. Once all the marbles were hit into the hole, the player with the most points won.

My sister and I collected industrial rubber bands as an adventure on our way around town. When enough bands were found we would play a game of rubber bands that involved using our fingers. The game is known as a Cat's Cradle or Origami in America. We always had other kids to play with. Another fun game I remember playing involved children gathered in a circle sitting around a symbol of a bowl dug into dirt and a collection of marbles or stones. We would take turns going around the circle tossing up the stones or marbles. The goal of the game was to try and gather as many marbles or stones from the bowl as possible before the end of the turn.

Little Girl Beautifully Broken

Dear Younger Self,
As a little girl who didn't understand the concept of the world around you, you learned to survive through your scars even though survival brought much loss.

     I have no memory of the connection and bond I had with my birth mom or dad. I was aware that dad was never around but had no grasp of why he was not there. What my mind was too young to comprehend at the time was the information I found in later years as I dug deeper into the research of my adoption. In fact, through The Ministry of Health and Social Welfare, I found the history of my mom and dad.

     With so much happening in my life there was little information given to me about my biological family. Already not knowing how to deal with the loss of family, what was to come next was least expected. The letter I received from The Ministry of Health and Social Welfare said that James Bryant, my birth father, had died of cholera in his hometown of Bong County, Liberia, on November 9, 2003. My birth father had been sick for quite some time. His occupation entailed being a farmer. Prior to the delivery of his two little girls James Bryant did not care about the well-being of our mamma, Siakor Weetor. From the time of his birth to that of his death, he contributed nothing to support his family.

My biological mom made an attempt to support and provide for us as she hustled trying to make a living. She spent her time selling whatever produce she could grow in her garden in the market. With the help of her family and community members, she was able to provide financial stability, but that income was not enough to sustain the life we needed. As a six-year-old girl I lacked an understanding of death. Grieving the loss of dad was hard when I did not comprehend what death was. Especially as death was an everyday thing where I grew up. I do not have any recollection of grieving the loss of our father. Trying to put a face to his name is impossible because I cannot. He was not present and I had to learn to be okay without him and to continue to carry on with our life. We were simply two little girls who were just kids.

I learned that my dad was not successful in his role as a husband and a father when his family needed him most. He failed our mom and his little girls, leaving us with no support of any kind. In addition, the family of James Bryant gave no financial support from the time of our birth up to now.

Dear Younger Self,
Your mamma invested her time by doing the best she could to make a living for her two little girls. Your Mamma could not make ends meet providing for you and your sister financially. With limited resources and lack of financial support she did what she thought was best and gave you up to the orphanage, hoping to provide a better life for you.

Although biological dad was a farmer, he was known for playing the flute in his hometown and for performing in nearby villages. The travel led to him keeping several "girlfriends" in each village. He also would come home frequently drunk, wasting any supporting money he may have contributed in helping raise his girls. He maintained such a lifestyle until the time of his death and my mom was left dealing with our care. Alone.

As of March 25, 2006, my sister and I resided with a PLAN foster mother, Femen. When we came into care and were taken for a medical checkup, it was found that my sister's health put her at risk for heart failure. She was treated with shots daily at a nearby clinic and was monitored for several weeks until her heart rate was back to normal. My sister could have died any day if Medicare had not been provided through the support and help of the adoption agency. We were taken to a hospital called Elway Hospital, as recorded in our case history by The Ministry of Health. After we were both examined, it was reported that we were suffering from malnutrition. Not only this, but blood tests were also drawn and The Ministry of Health and the tests concluded that my sister was severely anemic. Anemic to the point that she was in danger of severe health problems. The reports said that she was immediately given iron injections.

Case history completion by the Ministry of Health reported that there was no medical reason for her anemia. Being severely anemic caused her health care to continue to be monitored by a doctor, and other physicians, at Elway Hospital. She was suffering from a decrease in oxygen and a blood transfusion was needed to help improve her oxygen level. My sister was also suffering from malaria and hookworm as discovered in the report I read written by a Dr. McFadden on April 16, 2006.

Not being able to fully grasp everything that was going on with my sister, I was able to communicate with the doctors using my Liberian Pidgin. After weeks of her being monitored and treated professionally it was reported that she could have died. She pulled through with treatment and was able to eat and play with me again. With mamma struggling to provide for us and having limited resources to help my sister, mamma had the opportunity to contact PLAN when we were in foster care.

In March of 2006, our mamma was given three weeks to think about her option of putting us up for adoption. Before the three weeks arrived, she made the decision to put us up for adoption with the desire and hope that we would be given a better life. A brighter future.

Dear Younger Self,

Not having a mom or a dad around throughout this hard and exhausting journey, you continue to live knowing they aren't a part of your life and it has been challenging. Survival has cost you a tremendous amount of agony and loss. As loss endured, you had to come to terms with learning to accept that this was your new way of life. Without the presence or involvement of your mom and dad around you had had to fight your own battles. You and your sister walked through life protecting each other. After your transition in the hospital, you had no choice but to abandon the only home you knew and you entered into a new yet very different world.

Different Worlds

After Mom made the final decision to give up custody of us with the adoption agency, arrangements were made from The Ministry of Health to send over a representative who came to Gbargna to get us. Our case history was completed, and documents were made final. We were placed into foster care in Monrovia and placed for adoption. Who knew what the future held for us for our new life. Little did we know that as we distanced ourselves from life in Liberia to come to America, our world would change.

Miss Taylor, an American woman, came and took us out of Liberia to ensure our travel to America was safe. I remember getting off the airplane at the Portland International Airport. At that very moment, I wasn't sure about the emotions I felt. I was only a six-year-old girl facing a whole different world. Being in this large confusing environment of an airport, late at night, and seeing a crowd of people from a distance, not knowing that they were to soon be my new so-called family, made me feel lost. But this little girl was polite and kind. Even when confused because I was seeing people all around who looked nothing like me. Seeing a large group of people, soon to be family, for the first time was scary.

Dear Younger Self,
You and your sister have been taken from the only place you have ever known. Your world has flipped upside down in a flash.

How were two six year olds coming into a completely strange world, where home wasn't familiar, expected to react? Right there and then at the airport, we were introduced to our new family. Time was taken to visit with our new family and get to know everyone. I remember gifts of mini Polly Pocket doll collection sets were given out to me and my sister. We were surrounded by a large sum of people and it wasn't long before we were asked what we wanted our names to be. We were given the options of two names to choose from. Rebekah or Sarah. Who wanted to be Sarah and who wanted to be Rebekah? I

Our new life with the Henderson's included became Rebekah and my twin sister became Sarah. We were also asked what age we wanted to be. having four brothers and another sister who was Korean. All of the changes: a new family, a new environment, and a new language. My mind grew wary even when I was curious about what was going on. Everything happened in such little time that there was no room left to react, especially coming out of a war. My sister and I were left with no choice but to accept all that was transpiring without fully being able to comprehend what was happening. Back then, I wasn't able to put a name to the emotions that were transpiring because life circumstances changed so rapidly. Numbness is the term that I would have used if I had been older and more able to comprehend all of the changes.

Our new life became so different. The culture, the people, an indoor bathroom, shower, television, a warm house to live in, and a warm bed to sleep in made me adapt to this life faster than I had expected. The blankets we slept with were so soft that when I closed my eyes I slept in peace and comfort. Unafraid at night. Not having comforts prior, this new experience was eye awakening to me. It came as a shock to me that we didn't have to worry about not having enough food to eat, let alone not having to steal to sustain ourselves. Coming into this new world, we did not have to worry about our tummies being hungry and living off of one meal a day just to keep our fragile bodies from being sick. When we needed water to drink in Africa, we had to fetch it from the well, sometimes from a creek. Arriving in this new land we both have to worry about how we were going to fetch water or how far we had to go if we needed a drink of water. When we needed water it was right in front of us. My mind was in wonder and curiosity as I observed what was known as a kitchen. I was learning new terms and how things in America worked. Sometimes, looking into the fridge, I could not understand how so much food could be stored in a long box which kept food from rotting. I didn't understand how they were able to have a ton of food without running out. All that we didn't have back in Liberia was provided to us in America. There were so many different types of foods to eat. Already being a fan of fruit, I could eat all the fruit I wanted. I ate varieties of fruits which I had never eaten or heard of before; such as strawberries, raspberries, grapes, and blueberries. Fruit always managed to bring comfort and peace to my mind and it made my tummy happy.

Eating fruit wasn't the only thing that brought me happiness and a curious mind. I was adventuring with different ethnic foods that were unfamiliar to me. Other than rice and sardines and grass-hoppers and snails in my informer home, I had the opportunity to try new things. I tried foods such as pancakes, spaghetti, alfredo pasta, pizza, and various kinds of soups.

There we were, two six-year-old girls in a strange place, what was expected of us? We had to learn how to transition in this new life. We spent a lot of time playing with each other and our new broth-ers, cousins, and sister. We learned about jumping on a new play toy called a trampoline, playing on a swing set, and playing on a teeter totter. These new games brought me much joy, laughter and smiles.

The biggest change to me was seeing such busy streets with so many cars. Everywhere I looked, cars were traveling in multi-ple directions. I saw heavy traffic with both big and small vehicles. Traveling by vehicle brought a feeling of joy to my heart. I looked forward to always being ready to travel somewhere that wasn't the house. The lights on the streets shined so brightly in green, red, and yellow. My face would always light up seeing the colors shining so brightly reflecting on the car mirrors. Traveling safely with closed doors and safety belts was all new to me. Traveling long distances did not require walking everywhere we went. The change became an overwhelming and unsettling feeling for my six year old brain to accept. The honking of cars was loud and people weren't very kind on the road. Sometimes this feeling scared me and I didn't know what to think. I of the sat in silence, enjoying the ride, scenery, and listening to kids Bible songs.

It wasn't long before I was taught by my brothers how to ride a bike. Before getting on this bike, they modeled the bike riding method in order for me to catch on by riding on the flat surface of our driveway in a circle. They taught me to pedal and showed me how to break. I caught on rather quickly, faster than expected. It took me some time to adjust to the new experience. I would get on and off of the bike because I was fearful. I had no sense of balance or the idea of having to wear protective gear. Fear of falling took a lot of trust knowing that failure was going to happen. It took multiple practices watching my brothers and then learning from them. The more I practiced, the more I grew comfortable with the idea. Every chance I got to explore I would get excited to get outside. Once I got comfortable with how to balance, I would ride around the house from the driveway.

The other amazing piece of this new life was being able to engage with many different types of animals which I had never encountered before. Being in the presence of various animals lit up my face through smiles and giggles. We lived on a big piece of land with open space where horses, cats, dogs, rabbits, and chicken were available to hold and play with. Wild Life Safari introduced animals to me that I had not even seen in Africa. I had very little exposure to the scenery of Liberia as a little girl. Coming here, riding on a camel was such a fun experience even though I was frightened of heights. Seeing elephants and a pink bird called a flamingo was a sight to my six year old eyes. These were followed by a tiger and by hearing the roar of lions close.

It wasn't long before my sister and I became a part of the community through church events, church family members, and sports. We adapted to our new life rapidly. After settling into our new environment, meeting other children who looked nothing like me puzzled me a bit. We settled in at Salem First Baptist Church where the opportunity of friendship transpired. Meeting other children made me happy, even when the other children looked nothing like me and my sister. That fact didn't cloud my judgment and I played with them. They were all kids like me so I thought nothing of it. I made new friends. We adapted into this fresh and new environment and my sister and I connected with the church community through attendance at varied events.

One event, called AWANA (Approved Workmen Are Not Ashamed) occurred once a week, every Wednesday. AWANA was the start of experiencing religion. Other church families would come into a huge open community space and enjoy dinner meals. The event was a social gathering for church families to connect and engage with each other. Kids were expected to attend classes in classrooms where they would learn and recite as many Bible verses as possible. Rewards were winning medals. Personal rewards from our adoptive parents, if we recited many verses, were being able to choose where we would like to go for a treat whether it was Dairy Queen, Wendy's, or Burger King. Rewards were used to help motivate us. There were many other kids we would attend this event night with. Games involved running around in a circle competing against other kids and knocking down pins with bean bags. Teams were formed into color categories with leaders present by our side. It wasn't all about the fun and games because we were being taught how to pray and to read our Bibles at the same time.

As excited as I was to see new faces and meet other kids my age, I found it rather difficult to comprehend why kids went to class. So many children in big rooms with their mommies and daddies holding their hands. Sometimes I would wonder in my mind where my mommy and daddy were even though these mommies and daddies didn't look anything like us. My sister and I were given parents that didn't have our skin color and this puzzled me.

I wondered where my real mommy and daddy were. Home wasn't the same. There were no coconut trees, banana trees, or plum trees around me.

Dear Younger Self,

Childhood memories were mde fun for you with many games. Wii Games, board games, and card playing. Games you most definitely enjoyed were Mario Kart, Excite Truck, and Dance Revolution. Phase 10, Uno, Goldfish, and you enjoyed working on puzzles. You spent a lot of the time playing games and spent a lot of time with your brothers riding bikes. Playing on the playground lifted you up.

Family fun picnics were always something I looked forward to because it meant playing with cousins and riding bikes. Kids just being kids. I also looked forward to the holidays. Everyone gathering at Christmas, Thanksgiving, and Easter marked major celebrations. Christmas was a fun time for me growing up because the entire family would attend Sunday services where singing was involved. There were also various performances, spending time with family and friends, opening gifts, and dressing up. During these years time was spent outdoors in the summer, attending sport events and potlucks. Riding bikes around tracks in parks with my brothers, sisters, and cousins always made for a fun time. Not to mention, the adoption celebration created opportunities to meet and play with other adoptees. This potluck helped adopted children get to know each other, meet each other, and to learn our new names.

The adoption potluck brought people together with various choices of food that had been prepared. The gathering helped children connect with each other differently in social situations. Having these potlucks and seeing kids of my own color made me less alone. I could talk and communicate with the children openly, feeling unafraid to be myself. Each time the potlucks happened; I would get excited to the idea of seeing other kids like myself.

Other celebrations also meant a new experience in our new home. Thanksgiving meant feasting and giving thanks around the dinner table and playing games. Easter day was always a joy for me because of going over to Grandma's house and spending time with her while coloring eggs, easter egg hunting, and helping prepare meals. Playing games during the important holidays brought family together. When my siblings and I were young we were involved in a kids choir at the church. Plays were put on. Some of my brothers had lead roles in the plays and in choir. Sunday nights during evening service we would attend choir practices. I very much admire this part of my childhood with my brothers and sisters. We would put on plays, especially around Christmas time, when the sanctuary was full of people. I remember this part of my childhood happily. Later on, adolescent years also included social events through active participation in sports.

One of the most exciting memories of my life back then was attending my brother's baseball games. I purely enjoyed watching them run and play ball. I enjoyed going to their games and meeting new people. Watching my brothers play made me want to also play. Sooner than later my sister and I started to engage in playing sports just like our brothers, beginning with T-ball. As I began to grasp the game of T-ball and grew older. I learned the game of Basketball and Softball. I was actively involved in Softball. I also played Basketball through a certain age. My basketball coach was one of my older brothers. I played post as my main position but alternated to other positions. Sometimes playing left or right wing or point guard meant calling the shots and being the leader on the court. Basketball and Softball became my life as I grew older in the American culture.

In Softball I was coached by a family friend and I began building my skills in the athletic department. I was taught everything I needed as I learned practice skills, and learned the rules of fielding in the outfield, being an infielder, being a catcher, and the principles of having contact with the ball before swinging the bat. As my skills improved, I began playing and competing in tournaments. One memory that still resonates with me was when I broke my left wrist sliding into home plate with the referee calling me "safe!"

In that moment, an instant adrenaline rush made me cheerful until I began feeling pain on my left wrist which made it hard to get up from home plate. I attempted to get up but as soon as I felt extreme pressure on my wrist, I began weeping. The injury was so severe that the bones inside my wrist broke through. I was in so much pain that an ambulance was called and I was taken to a hospital immediately. I remember that day as though it were yesterday. I went into surgery where screws were placed into my wrist to hold things into place. For weeks, I was in a cast which made schooling and homework very difficult.

Over the years things gradually changed where I began traveling more with my softball team to compete in tournaments. When Basketball ended, Softball was it's replacement and became what I stuck with until I was fifteen years old. I always traveled with a team of players who I would attend games with. The many years that I played, we even won some tournaments, were great memories. I keep these memories with me because I really enjoyed playing and competing against other players, earning medals, and different forms of awards, throughout the tournaments.
Third base was where I started and eventually I worked my way up to a catching position that I held for years. Catching was a ton of work, calling out plays and staying in communication with my team on the field. Throughout these games I remained right-handed because it was my dominant hand. As growth continued, coaches started to train me to hit left-handed. I wasn't sure how I was going to adjust to the new change, but I did. Over time, I gradually grew comfortable with hitting with my left and I stuck with it for quite some time. It was almost as though I had forgotten how to swing a bat with my right hand. Once I started swinging left-handed it remained.

I remember not only being active in Softball and Basketball games. I also remember vacation trips with my family during the summer. Family fun vacation trips to Disneyland with friends and camping trips to Triangle Lake would take place around September due to the birthday celebrations of my Korean sister and our adoptive dad. Triangle Lake memories included canoeing, throwing the frisbee around, camping out, and socializing with different family and church group members. Other fun vacation times entailed a visit to Canada, Washington, and roller coaster theme parks. Vacation trips were spent visiting with long distant cousins, uncles, and aunts.

When we would make trips to Canada, we would stop at a theme park called Silverwood where we would enjoy riding roller coasters and playing in the water theme park. I adored the theme parks, the camping trips, and visits up to Canada to see aunts, uncles, and cousins. Visits to Washington were also memories I will cherish because of the State Fair which included watching the horse barrel races, eating moo-witches, looking at animals in the stable barn, riding on a boat out to sea, crabbing, taking walks along the beach, picking blackberries for berry cobblers and smoothies, enjoying the hot tub, and going on various rides.

Disneyland, Silverwood, and attending the State Fair always gave me something to look forward to. The Washington State Fair made my day due to the hypnotist shows, where open space was provided for many people to gather around, sit, and enjoy the gal hypnotizing people. The hypnotist was always the highlight of going to the Washington State Fair. After our summer trips up to Washington we would come back home the night before Sunday Service for Church in the park. Being away from home on adventures protected my sister and I from increasing trouble in our adoptive home.

As summer continued, July and August brought enjoyment through Sunday church Service at Riverfront Park in Spokane, WA. These services brought people together to be in the presence of worship. Church was always a way for me to get out and socialize with peers. It was a call for dressing up, singing, listening to music, engaging in social activities with my peers, and enjoying potlucks. Attending the youth group involved planning events for middle and high schoolers. These church events were held in campgrounds, and we would be gone for a week. We went to these church events to learn more about God through the development of relationships with other Christian kids, playing games, spending time in the Word, and singing hymns.

We also attended a Christian event that included the participation of mothers and their daughters. Young women came together for not only fellowship, but to become the best godly women that can be after attending a public conference. Being given the chance and opportunity to attend the conference made me appreciative of the fellowship built for women and their daughters. When I started attending, I thought I was going there to be a support since my adoptive mom was attending with family friends and their daughters. The conference encouraged me to build on other relationships and friendships with people. It wasn't till I was older, when problems in the home began that I started rejecting my family's way of Christianity. I was never encouraged once mistakes were made. As I became older, I began to comprehend what was going on in our home through the religion of Christianity. I felt suffocated as though no wrong could be done or forgiven. While much of the teaching "comes from the Bible," my situation at home made me rethink a lot of my own personal beliefs.

I began to question what they considered being Christian and the answers I found only hurt me more. The belief system felt all wrong as my adoptive parents manipulated teachings in order to abuse power by inflicting pain on me and my sister. Things didn't sit right with me when I started seeing my adoptive parents for who they were. They presented themselves as Godly folks but behind the scenes they were dangerous. In response to the teaching of what a Christian is, I would get into heated arguments with my adoptive mom. I felt belittled in their idea of religion as they were getting away with emotional, physical, and mental abuse in our home. I grew angry and felt betrayed and unloved in yet another home which proved unsafe. The relationship I had with them was destroyed.

The practices they inflicted in the name of Christianity were the complete opposite of what they would preach to us kids. I caught on to the wrong- doings that they held to control me. A fire was stirred in me due to the way my sister and I were treated at home. I was forced to only allowed wear clothing that symbolized what the religion required, rather than being taught who I am in Christ. All of the lists of social rules that were created upset me and I began fighting back through verbal aggression.

The true characters of my adoptive parents only showed behind the walls of home. While in public, they would hold themselves as if we were living the perfect life. Not in reality. Reality turned into nightmares and abuse. Rules of conduct were everything to them so I had very little choice in the matter. I obeyed in their rules until I started going my own way. I was confused living the ideology of Christianity and what was being taught to me. While my sister and I were being abused in a family we had no choice being part of, they faked their true character in the public's eye. Hearing how grateful and blessed that I should be and that I had great parents while they were hurting us in silence brought on more hardship.

My own experience regarding their religious beliefs did not come easy to me. It hurt me really badly. My sister and I could not say anything while we were being abused by this family that called themselves Christian. Our journey became complicated and long. This journey became the worst experience possible for adoptees who thought we would be loved and nurtured with compassion and kindness. Being young and feeling trapped by this family did not bring any kind of comfort or peace to my well-being, personal growth, and development as a young American woman.

Religion was the leading focus as we became older and there was limited option but to engage and participate in social event in the church called CYIA (Christian Youth in Action). Kids from different communities who were a part of this social Baptist movement went out to spread the Word of God to lost souls. I do remember being asked if I wanted to do this and I was very hesitant about wanting to join. Regardless, I was volunteered by my adoptive mom. It didn't matter what my response was, I was stuck doing this thing that I already was in question of.

CYIA was held five days a week during Bible Clubs at playgrounds and other churches. Just like CYIA, ministry work played a

Behind These Walls

When my sister and I were younger things felt peachy with summer vacation trips, church events, sports, and making connections through family and friends. Hardships came along and the environment my sister and I lived in became toxic and turned into an abusive household. Again, we were thrown into a situation and not knowing what to expect from the family we had been adopted by changed everything. Puberty hit and changed the game even more. Our home no longer had our best interests at heart, so we began struggling. Growing up the way we did and being raised by our adoptive family now became a living hell for me. Encountering womanhood at an early age made living that much harder.

The people who were supposed to create a safe and secure environment failed to do so and once again I did not feel unconditional love, protected, encouraged, or supported by this family. All of this destroyed me over time. Without trust, once again I lived in fear. I did not know what a menstrual cycle was when I experienced my first cycle at eight or nine years old. I remember the first time it happened, I was a bit freaked out and scared thinking that I was dying. I didn't understand what was happening with my body so I screamed and started to cry.

Adoptive Mom heard me and came rushing in to find out what the commotion was. She was aware of what transpired and helped me take care of the situation. I reached womanhood sooner than what was expected. For me, it was terrifying seeing so much blood and I had no understanding of what that meant. I started to go through changes. I became moodier and had attitude all around. Growing pains really set things into motion that lead to things getting worse at home. Life became a bit more challenging and difficult. With all the changes going on inside of me, emotions started to form as well. I didn't truly understand what was happening to me physically and emotionally. Mood swings from highs to lows were confusing to me.

For awhile, when I wasn't experiencing the pain of womanhood, I enjoyed my life. A lot of my free time when homeschooled, consisted of dancing, listening to music, watching a favorite movie or show, being outside in the sun, dressing up, singing, shopping, and pretending to model in front of my digital camera. Times were great when I had personal time to myself. Personal time became the happiest place for me when I needed space.

Personal time also marked the start of things getting tougher. I remember being downstairs in the basement alone on the computer one day, innocently searching up hip hop dance videos. I saw an ad pop up to the right of the computer screen. Curiosity sparked and when ads popped up. This time curiosity presented itself through naked people. Keep in mind that I couldn't comprehend anything that was going on within myself much less the echo in my ears that sin was bad. I was never communicated with regarding what porn was or about any sexual matters. Clicking on the various ads intrigued my eyes through the visuals, yet I found it confusing. I attended youth group at church and the youth pastor touched base on sex. My young mind didn't comprehend what that meant going through so much change in my youth years. I grew curious about the meaning of this word and sat through an entire lecture of how sex was only meant to happen between a woman and her husband. Sex was bad. This was the only thing I learned that night.

Youth group kids weren't taught anything else about safety or what it really meant and I was lost. I wasn't getting the lesson from home so I directed my own way around the word sex. I looked it up and would find peers from school to talk with, not from home. I went to a specific peer to ask questions because I felt comfortable asking her.

I saw that she was living a life with rules which didn't control her or hold her down from experiencing natural teenage hormones. She described sex as fun. My peer did not go into depth about what sex was but when she stated it was fun that's all my mind gathered. So, I left that social engagement with the idea of fun. After the class with the youth pastor examining, and not really examining, sex I started doing my own research in whatever way that looked like. Mainly, I went through Google and experimented on myself. The further I began looking into ads, the more my mind started to slowly record what I was seeing through this screen. A routine began where if I was done with my homework, I would sneak downstairs to the basement and look up what I saw.

I became addicted and obsessed with wanting to feel some sort of love that would help me escape the reality of home. Disengaging became very difficult. I didn't know how to turn back to stop what was going on each day in the basement watching those videos. Daily, I would experiment with what I watched in the video on myself. I would search up different keywords that resembled what was being shown to me through videos and I came across multiple ideas with very vivid images that could not escape from my mind. I didn't understand the concept of addiction. I was not familiar with the word. I was exposed to the images early without being ready. I was very confused and scared. In fact, being scared caused me so much worry knowing that if my parents found out I would be in big trouble. I kept the secret to myself for months.

I navigated my way through the computer system to try to find a way to hide what I was looking at so no one would find out. I steered through settings and found something that said" delete search engine" so I clicked and the search history was deleted. Once I was able to navigate my way through the system settings, I became an expert at protecting myself by hiding and deleting the videos of porn so I wouldn't get in trouble. I was scared of opening up to my adoptive parents. The discomfort I felt was not enough to go talk to my adoptive parents. I got away with what I was doing and continued exploring and experimenting on myself when I was alone. Different levels of emotions felt through the roof already and I did not know how to manage the overwhelming emotions and thoughts that I was experiencing.

I continued with daily activities through social gatherings, such as school, and Friday events called PE. PE was a once-a-week activity where other homeschoolers would go to the church and hang out in the gym to play games. PE was the only source of interaction we had. Sometimes in the summer, we would go produce picking fruits and vegetables on various farms with close family friends. We would pick boxes and boxes of grapes and help can grape juice. We had a variety of options to pick from. We picked bell peppers, tomatoes, and onions, and would help make salsa. We also picked peaches, strawberries, blueberries, raspberries, and black berries. I had never seen so much fruit during my entire life in Africa. My love for fruit started there and grew even more when I came to America. This part of me has not changed.

I was keeping up my appearance in public and back at home as there was no way of telling anyone. That part of my life remained hidden. As weeks and months went by, I wasn't doing well and I would lash out and act out at my adoptive parents who didn't understand why I would act very differently some days. Mood swings were all over the place. Between twelve and fourteen my emotions got out of control. One night I went into my adoptive parents' bathroom in the dark and just wept in agony. I could not stop crying. My adoptive mom happened to be home that night and heard me crying in their bathroom. She came in and asked what was wrong. With everything I was going through with them, it took much courage to communicate with her openly and honestly. I did not have the ability to come to terms with and talk about all of the overwhelming emotions I was experiencing without exposing myself and what I was doing even though I was confused and felt so alone in my head. She asked if something happened to me or if someone touched me as I cried. She repeated that question and I got to the point where I just told her that I was touched. She asked me immediately when this happened and told her that it was in Liberia. While telling her what happened in Liberia played a role in my personal development, I did not feel comfortable enough to tell her the other thing that was going on with me. I was too scared of the consequences and what the punishment would be so I kept the porn use a secret for quite some time. When I told her about my sexual abuse, she hugged me. It was difficult getting to that point where I could express myself. We may have shared a connection in the moment, but nothing changed. No action was taken to help me after opening up about my sexual abuse in Liberia. I continued to suffer and struggle severely, in silence.

I had a crush on a youth leader, at age twelve, and it became my distraction when I was going through a hell of a transition and stuffing it all down inside hoping to escape somehow. My hormones were all over the place and I was unaware of why because of a lack of education. During this time of change, not having a father figure hit me harder than what was to be expected. The fixation I had on the youth pastor was the start of sexual fantasies which led to an addiction that I wasn't aware of at the time.

I recall attending an evening service one Sunday with a guest speaker who was also going to talk on the matter of sex. I was sitting with my parents and one of my brothers. I was confused even after exploring through the internet so I turned to my second oldest brother, whispered, and asked what sex was. His response was to ask Mom and Dad. Well, asking him left me feeling defeated at the thought of warming up to my adoptive parents to ask that question, so I just didn't bother.

As I've gotten older, being able to reflect more deeply about my own personal growth over the years without the family has brought me a long way. Things from adolescent years to teenage years became very unstable for me. I received my first phone when I turned fifteen. Looking forward to the excitement of owning a phone brought joy, followed by triumph. However, having a phone only made the sexual cravings stronger which revealed opportunities for me. Not understanding the vocabulary at the time, "masturbation" took place. During what I estimate was four months hooked on porn, I would act on my feelings as a coping mechanism when I needed to escape from reality.

When stress became overwhelming or I felt unhappy in the home, porn was the tool I went to. I isolated myself and began withdrawing. I had implemented something into my life that I couldn't understand due to how repressed my parents were. So I left the thoughts in my mind to process on my own. My parents did not make it easy to be approachable. I felt suffocated and convinced myself that they would not understand. We girls were told by adopted mom and dad that if we ever had issues we could talk to them. But their actions did not give me the assurance that they were welcoming and inviting. Teenage years became so unstable for me that I fell into a major depression, whether or not my parents were aware of it, ignorance kept them from helping me when I really needed them.

I thought that after telling my adoptive Mom I was sexually abused she would have opened her eyes to getting me help. That wasn't the case. I carried on and the depression continued. The addiction to porn began to grow as sexual gratification was all I had left to continue surviving in that house. With the religion my parents were putting into practice, I felt judgment all around, so I stayed silent.

The largely conservative and repressed environment I lived in limited my experiences as a teenager, a tremendous setback for me. The addiction of porn along with natural transitioning to womanhood taxed my mental and emotional health and I started to keep myself locked up in my room. Why? Because my room was the only safe space I had. Home definitely did not bring me any form of security, safety or happiness. I wanted an escape out of the environment I was in but couldn't find one. My adoptive family lacked the necessary skills in providing emotional support. During this time the discipline and punishment that was displayed increased, yet continued to be kept a secret in order to keep up appearances with other Christian friends and families. Adoptive Dad expressed at one point that he did not appreciate the idea of other folks stepping into his parental role. This was a loss within itself because everything that could go wrong was going wrong.

I wasn't much of a believer in counseling which burned another bridge. What hope did I have of anyone believing me if I explained what my sister and I had experienced behind closed doors. Complications were everywhere and left me fighting my own battles. One particular struggle in my home life was my failing grades. Being homeschooled with seven other siblings did not have a very positive impact on my self-esteem, which had a direct impact on my feeling of self-worth.

Low self-esteem manifested itself in the form of addictive behavior, particularly sexual gratification and caused my mental state to fall to a point where I thought life was not worth living anymore. Struggling with my emotions, as mentioned before, my adoptive parents, who again were very conservative and religiously repressed, chose to ignore to my problems. When I was dealing with poor behavioral control, they would pretend nothing was wrong and in order to cope and I withheld communicating my feelings because I felt my struggles were not being validated.

I was in misery and not being a biological daughter to these people made me feel as though my problems did not matter, which caused further emotional pain. School overwhelmed me making it extremely hard to focus. The discipline and inappropriate punishment happening in our home felt like hate to me which deepened my brokenness, my wounds, and my scars. My adoptive mom's sister and brother-in-law became aware of the toxicity with my parents and got involved. The fight I put up with my adoptive family led to my aunt and uncle wanting to adopt me.

Consequently, I remember walking into a private room of the First Baptist Church with my parents, myself, the pastor, and my uncle and aunt. We went to the church to discuss matters that my aunt and uncle found troubling. The goal of everyone meeting was to try and figure out a resolution to the problems that were going on at home. My uncle and aunt were trying to save me from anything more severe but the meeting was a losing battle. After that, my mom and her sister went their separate ways. Nothing was resolved and I went back home being more miserable than I already was. The environment was so unstable and unhealthy for me that I had no other choice but to continue struggling with trying to deal with sexual urges on my own.

Struggling in all areas of life at the most vulnerable stage in life left me feeling even more alone. My adoptive parents discipline was extreme and I lashed out in verbal aggression. Lash outs included things like; "I hate you guys," "I don't want to live here," "I'm not happy here," "I wish I had different parents," "I would be better off without you guys," and so forth. I had moments where I would lash out by yelling or screaming.

There were many moments where I would cry out for my aunt when I was in distress. I wanted to escape that environment so bad but had no way of doing so. With no other way out, I also acted out with physical with aggression when both my adoptive mom and dad would not back off when asked. My adoptive mom decided to push boundaries further and she would get up in my face yelling and even spitting in my face if she was eager for answers.

I would ask that she back off, but she wouldn't. She had a tendency not to listen during heated moments so I would do what I could to push her away from me. I didn't particularly like confrontation let alone having someone being up in my face. Hell, I put up a fight. During those moments my adoptive dad had the audacity to back her up even when he knew that she was in the wrong. If she asked me a question and I chose to not respond, I felt justified. My refusal to speak infuriated my adoptive parents even more, to the point where they felt they had the right to put their hands on me. They used the Bible to convince themselves that they were in the right all the time. One verse that would be recited to me "Children obey your parents in the Lord for this is right."

Their words were something I would have to listen to and it made me want to fight back more when they chose not to back away from me. I felt pushed into a corner where resisting the urge to fight back was impossible. Religion seemed to be the priority and

focus on the home and I refused to just let them get away with the wrong doings. They would justify using the Bible against me for obedience and I would justify my behavior through silence.
The toxic relationship with both adoptive parents had a negative impact healthy development as I was transitioning into womanhood.

During this time, I felt as though I wasn't seen as a daughter. I started having issues trying to rationalize the idea and thought that I was loved. A lot of emotions and feelings about being loved by my adoptive family brought issues on with my Korean sister. I felt that she was seen as more of a daughter than me because she did no wrong. In their eyes, she was the golden child. Even if she did something wrong, she flew under the radar. So, this was another situation in which I struggled and I brought my feelings to my adoptive mom's attention.

I remember simply asking if she loved my Korean sister more than me. Her response was," I love all my kids the same" and it was left like that. That conversation and the response to my question left me numb on top of numb. Growing up in a family of girls and boys, I had issues when it came to reinforcement concerning religion. The girls were expected to cover themselves up in long dresses and skirts. Wearing jeans and a shirt was out of the question when it came to Sunday service. But jeans and shirts were able to be worn throughout evening service. Rules seemed to be different for my Korean sister than for me and my sister. I felt like it was mainly me because I tended to push rules and boundaries with our adoptive parents because why was I going to listen to them if they didn't listen to me. I was known as the rebellious child which I became because I just started not caring anymore.

My family, so called family, started to mean nothing to me. When it came to wardrobes on Sundays and looking our Sunday best, those were boundaries I pushed. There were times where I would walk out of the house on Sundays wearing something either short or revealing and I would immediately get scolded. I would have to go back inside and change. When it came to my Korean sister those rules did not seem to apply to her. Why was it I had to put up fights when I could plainly observe that there was a difference in how my sister, and I were treated. The relationship with my adoptive parents was flawed and the way I was treated did not bring me a sense of peace. I don't remember experiencing genuine love. My adoptive parents loved us in the way they thought was best, but it wasn't the type of love I needed. I felt that they never made me feel as though I was enough and I had to figure out how to keep going and living through all of the pain.

When I became upset, mad, irritable, and angry I tended to act out in aggression. I would slam doors, kick doors, and throw my own personal belongings without a care in the world. These outbursts led to verbal aggressiveness and attitude issues. My mouth was known for getting me into trouble. All of the verbal and physical aggression, the arguments, the attitude, and boundary pushing were not because I was seeking out attention. I feel strongly that my parents were instigators in many situations specifically to get reactions out of my sister and me.

Silent Battles

While I received my first phone at age fifteen, it didn't take long before I lost it. I had it for only a couple months. Struggling with the porn use without the awareness of my adoptive parents was a disease I was trying to fight through. Having a phone became a burden in regard to keeping my secret hidden. I went to a youth pastor to talk to him about my struggle, hoping that he would help steer me in the right direction. We chatted and I was willing to open up to him about my porn addiction. He was responsive and asked me questions and just encouraged me to talk to my parents. I spent weeks after that conversation trying to figure out how I was going to face the truth and tell at least one of my parents. My head was spinning. I wanted to come clean.

I spent lots of restless nights sleeping, mourning, and grieving for various reasons. After weeks of examining my options I just wanted to get things off my chest so they would stop eating me up. Lying awake one day in my bed, I decided it was time. I got out of the bed, went into the living room, and asked my adoptive Mom if she had the time so I could talk with her. Keep in mind, my heart was racing. Not knowing what to expect when I was exposed myself was terrifying. She followed me down the hall into the bedroom.

I slowly worked up the courage to let it out. It took some time but the truth came out. I told her that I was struggling with porn and that I had been for quite some time. She freaked out and her voice raised. She asked why over and over again. I was asked to hand over my phone and I did. Not sure what going on inside her head, I could see she was concerned which may be why she freaked. It's the only rational explanation I could come up with. After bringing up the topic about my porn use I just recall standing there. I don't remember her saying much after that. She left the room. I find it bizarre but a couple weeks after that, my Korean sister was given my phone.

There was no real resolution to the problem after I told my adoptive mom. I don't recall going into counseling immediately after the confession that night. I'm sure there was talk about my addiction. I never saw that phone again. The worst of it all wasn't the phone being taken away but the fact that the youth leader whom I spoke with avoided acknowledging my presence. When he saw me, there was no effort put in to try and converse with me after I had shared something very vulnerable to him. This left me walking on eggshells.

Already feeling alienated from this family, I was reminded that my sister and I had already lost so much of who we were. Losing the only home we were familiar with, our community, our daily routine, our freedom, was bad enough. The major loss of them all was our birth Mom, the woman who sacrificed it all, hoping the best for her two girls. She gave us up to provide protection, safety, love, and a better life just so we could experience abuse over and over again.

I question my adoptive parents choice to adopt us to do right by their religious faith. They couldn't even see how manipulative they were acting and used the Bible as an excuse for their behavior. It appeared to me that my adoptive parents didn't take into consideration our history and the background we were coming from. One time, at six-years-old, my hair was being done by our

adoptive mom and I sat on that living room floor telling her the story of the war that happened. I told her how soldiers came into the village and started shooting people and tying people up.
I'm not sure what part of a six-year-old girl telling her story about a war she was just experienced did not resonate with her. I was gaslit many times regarding how I should be grateful for having a roof over my head. I was called a brat by one of my brothers one night and I could not help but react by stomping away and crying. They were unaware and unwilling to see the reality of the wrong that was done to my sister and met.

My acting out was a cry out for help but that message wasn't taken seriously when I was being judged and being looked upon as a problem child. Putting a roof over someone's head does not make you a good parent. That was one of my thoughts throughout this misery of hell. I have always wondered if my adoption was just for their own satisfaction and to prove to their Christian families and friends that they were doing God's work. When kids are being abused in their own home, it isn't God's work. My adoptive parents treated adoption as ministry so that two little girls could be saved instead of simply loved. We were saved, but not in the way that was truly needed. I didn't feel like I was living. I felt more like a prisoner as they tried to control who we were, where we came from, our heritage, background, and history. Our trauma was not accepted nor were we given the help needed to heal.

Every negative emotion I had brought so much frustration, anger, irritability, and disappointment. They lacked the capacity to examine the situation more closely because it was complex in all the ways one can imagine. They had very high expectations and when those expectations weren't met they become even more controlling. I was the disobedient child who didn't listen to the rules of the house. I concluded that my life went deeper than just following rules and instead of compliance, I took on more abuse.

I would ask how our adoption came to be and was told that my parents met a couple at a Volcanoes game where the topic of adoption came about. This couple and my adoptive parents were engaged in the conversation and the names of an agency was given to my parents. From here, my adoptive parents investigated the agency and heard about two six-year-old girls needing to be adopted into a loving and caring home.

My adoptive parents went online and saw photos of us. My adoptive mom wanted to adopt and that's precisely what happened. Not only this, but my Korean sister wanted twin sisters for her birthday. That wish was granted. All the time we were being gaslit by my older brother who told us that she would cry out for her mom every night. In a moment that I was feeling that my sister and me were being treated differently than our Korean sister, this was a moment when I wanted to try and bond on a deeper level with my brother. So, one Sunday morning with him I tried to connect with him as he drove the car. I wasn't heard so I just stopped engaging with him. I just rode with him to church that Sunday in silence. This situation was also a leading cause to why I emotionally checked out, distancing myself any way I could from this family.

Once again, we lost the meaning of family. My sister and I unfortunately suffered from the actions of this family. I found it difficult considering these people our family when "family" wasn't what this family was about. Both adoptive parents were abusive in their own way. My adoptive dad was a disciplinarian. When he didn't understand how to deal with any the girls, he kept himself at a distance. Specifically, he didn't know how to parent or deal with me and my sister. His method of discipline was intolerable. There was more than one occasion where I feared him. When he got angry, he got physically aggressive with his hands. For example, one night I heard my sister crying and screaming in her room and I immediately got up from the living room to see what was happening because I was scared.

When I peeked into my sister's bedroom I found my adoptive dad standing on her leg with force and pressure. While my adoptive mom was sitting on top of her. I could not bear what I saw when I heard my sister cry. I did not take a liking to what was happening, so I tried fighting my way into the room, freaking out, and yelling at them to get off her. They continued what they were doing to her and I was told to go back to the living room but I just could not get myself to listen to anything they were instructing me to do. I did not tolerate their actions. It was upsetting to me to see and hear my sister in pain and they had the nerve to threaten me because I wasn't obeying.

Another memory I recall is when my sister rebelled against wearing make-up. We were treated as though wearing make-up was a crime. There were various occasions where they punished my sister by not allowing her to order meals when we went out with the family. She was restricted from restaurant meals unless she apologized for her disobedience. I experienced the same thing. I was punished most often because of my attitude and disobedience. Our parents would tell the other kids that they weren't allowed to speak to either one of us if we didn't say we were sorry.

The mistreatment continued. Often, If neither one of us were ready to be obedient and follow their rules the punishment was longer. My sister and I were at different points in our life with this family but we both experienced being locked in our rooms without access to food. We would immediately be alienated from eating with the family in the dining room. There were times where we would be forced to come eat with the family when we were upset because they'd been unfair and abusive. That's something I personally had a problem with. Throughout this difficult time with family meals, our parents had us kids keep a Bible with us at the dining room table to reflect on scripture. After the scripture was read, we would be quizzed about what was just said. I became so depressed that I had moments where I would starve myself and keep myself isolated away in my room.

Sometimes I would go into the kitchen and sneak a handful of chocolate chips or whatever else I could find without waking anyone up. A vivid memory that will forever remain with me is one night when I was forced to stay in my room and wasn't allowed to come out to go to the bathroom. My adoptive mom refused to let me go and I was forced to hold in my pee throughout the night. Consequently, I urinated on myself and on the carpet. She came to check up on me and noticed that the carpet was wet, so she decided to take me out and bring me into the living room. She sat me down while I still had very soaked socks on my feet. I remember being faced towards the front door. She tied my hands and tied my own pee sock around my mouth and I sat there for some time. Everything after that morning and throughout the day is blank in my mind.

Another memory is when I decided one day to go into the kitchen and grab any picture magnets of me that were on the side of refrigerator. I took them all down. I was aware that this home wasn't really a home. I was fed up and grew weary tolerating the abuse. I was losing sight of the fact that I was part of a family, knowing that they did not truly care about me. I was told that I should be grateful by Christian friends and families who knew very little of what happened behind closed doors. My adoptive dad noticed that my softball magnets were gone and immediately came to me. Furious. He asked me where they were and I played it off as though I didn't have them but could see he was adamant about getting the magnets back. I kept on refusing and he stormed, demanding them.

My mind was so conflicted about this family. I was considered part of the family but treated like crap. At some point, sooner than later I ended up giving up the magnets to him. He went into the kitchen and hung them back up. Not long after, he stormed back furiously asking if I had any other magnets and I responded "no" because I gave him all that there was. This situation spiraled out of control and created unnecessary drama. Things got out of hand when shouted at him to get out and he didn't. The next thing I knew, he started taking personal belongings away from me as a form of punishment.

My adoptive mom stood there observing by the door watching it all. She wasn't there to defend me. This was me, once again, in a power struggle with both parents and eventually a brother trying to intervene. I was so infuriated that I began shouting and screaming at everyone to get out and to leave me alone. My request created a bigger mess out of the situation.

There was no winning, never was with them. I remember grabbing the cordless phone that was on my dresser. I chucked it out of my room. The phone ended up flying towards my adoptive mom and it hit her. It wasn't my intention to have that happen but it did. My adoptive dad decided he was going to come into my room and put his hands on me. I had no choice but to fight him off when he became enraged. The next thing I recall is trying to fight him off me while on the built-in couch bed. It was very difficult. I was being attacked so of course I fought back. I wanted to be left alone but that wasn't happening. Some of my belongings ended up on the floor because when I get angry I tend to throw my stuff. I had scissors in my room that I used to cut jeans and old t-shirts. My adoptive mom was never a fan of me doing that in my personal time. Creating style was something that made me smile. My adoptive mom had a habit of going into my room regularly and taking things. I would notice were missing and that would just set me off, irritable.

The scissors were in reach of my adoptive dad. While on top of me, he grabbed them and said these exact words, "I'm going to stab her with this." My adoptive mom witnessed the scene. One of my brothers came into the room as I was putting up a fight because my adoptive dad would not get off me. The fact that there were scissors in his hands was bad enough. I needed him to get him off me. My brother joined in, trying to restrain me from the kicking and punching I was doing. The presence of that brother also didn't help the state of mind I was in. I remember trying to fight him off also. I was held down against my own will and in the chaos it got to a point where giving up was all I could do. I didn't have the strength or the energy to continue fighting.

My adoptive dad and brother eventually got off me when I surrendered fighting against them. As a form of punishment my personal belongings were taken out of my room after that fight, and I was finally left alone. The only way I could get my things, like jewelry and hemmed clothing, was if I was obedient. For a few weeks after this event occurred I did what I needed to get my belongings back. I approached my adoptive mom, asking her if I could get my stuff back. Her response was "no" because my attitude hadn't changed when in fact I had done well for a whole week straight. My improved behavior didn't matter to her. Living with abuse that was on going. I never understood why my sister and I were mistreated while our abusers were not being held responsible for their actions.

Even today, at twenty-two, I can't understand it.

There were times where I was dragged by my arms out of the bunk beds we girls had because I would refuse to obey. Punishment was given over the pettiest things. On multiple occasions I was forced into joining family dinners and I would refuse. Having dinner with the family was the last thing I wanted. Sitting around the table, reading scripture with ignorance to the abusive situation in the home was a toxic event. These dinners continued over the days and weeks. I refused attending family meals because I wasn't going to tolerate the treatment. I couldn't bear to look at any of my family members. Surrounding myself with a family I hated was uncomfortable. I was often in a bad mood and angry with my adoptive mom or adoptive dad and sometimes my siblings. I would get up out of my seat and attempt to get away from any of them.

Sometimes I would not ask permission and would just to get up and leave, making my way to my room. When they were done with the family dinner, I would wait until I felt comfortable enough to come out and feed myself. My adoptive mom would question what I was up to. I would answer her with ``I'm hungry" and her response would be, "Dinner was already offered." I would avoid certain family meals at the table in order to find the only peace I could. I avoided engaging with anyone. If I wasn't allowed to eat I would wait until night time to sneak into the kitchen and gain access to the chocolate chips that were either stored in a cupboard or in a jar on the counter. The abuse began soon after my sister and I were adopted.

I wasn't much older than six-years-old when I would wet the bed at times. I would let adoptive mem know what happened and I went into the bathroom with her to get cleaned off. Sometimes the punishment for wetting the bed was being forced to take a cold shower. I would stand there and just start screaming and crying and my step mom would make sure that I stayed under the cold running water. Cruelty in punishment with them was always blown out of proportion. If it wasn't one thing, it was another. If I wasn't dealing with my adoptive mom I would surely deal with my adoptive dad.

I don't remember exactly how old I was or what the following event happened, but I was old enough that it sticks with me to this day. The family was upstairs and I was down in the basement. I recall sitting in the closet of my adoptive mom and dad's room in the dark and in a very intense emotional state. The only noise I remember is the family laughing and having a good time. I heard someone coming down the stairs as laughter continued and for some reason I was crying hard. I remember sitting in the closet in the dark knowing that my adoptive dad was coming closer and he was wearing a mask that frightened me. This mask looked like a monster. I was in tears and screaming but it didn't stop him. He just continued. After this game, which I did not find humorous, I went back upstairs dismayed at what I heard. When my adoptive dad went back upstairs my family members were laughing.

My adoptive dad had a temper and he was aggressive with the animals he met if they misbehaved, or for no reason at all. My sister had a white cat named Star. One day my adoptive dad snapped, grabbed her cat, and threw it across the driveway from the dining room. Situations like this made it apparent that something wasn't right with this family. The worst part of the experience was feeling trapped. Other times I remember adoptive dad would aggressively rub my dog's nose into urine on the carpet. I found my adoptive dad's behavior unacceptable. For these reasons, I kept myself distant from him.

Even our case worker only came to visit us once. We never heard from her again. The more abused I felt, the quieter and lonelier I got. My adoptive dad was an aggressive man who did not know how to properly manage his anger. When he was enraged, I would fear him. There were times when I was afraid for my sister's life when he was abusive towards her.

Being in public with him stirred up a lot of uncomfortable emotions. When my sister had to go places with him alone I wanted to go with them because I saw how he would treat her. I should not have to be forced into a home environment where I feared my parents. Frankly, no kid should have to fear their parents. I found my adoptive dad's behavior unacceptable. For these reasons, I kept myself distant from him.

Adoptive dad believed his way of parenting and going about handling business was right. The reality was that he had failed as a father because he wasn't willing to change. one time, my adoptive parents, myself, and my sister were going to take a visit up to California to visit my oldest brother when he went into the army. The night prior to leaving for California I had my suitcase packed and ready to go. The morning, we were leaving I remember taking my luggage out to the van to load the vehicle. I was struggling a bit trying to get my suitcase in the back. I had my Australian dog with me outside, at the time, on a leash. As I was packing my things into the van, I heard this loud screech as though it was a cry. It got me worried, so I went over to my dog, near the vehicle, and saw that my adoptive dad was over there.

I dropped what I was doing, and I remember seeing my dog in fear. When he abused our animals, it felt like a personal attack. I asked my adoptive dad what he had done, and he didn't answer. I took my dong, Sparky, and brought him with me, holding the leash so I could finish getting my luggage into the vehicle. I was struggling to fold the seat down so I could fit it in the back seat. My adoptive dad, on the other side of the vehicle, saw me struggling. He came over in a nonchalant way, standing behind me, and then grabbed the leash as I was hanging onto it. Instead of offering help to me he decided anger was the solution.

He yanked the dog leash and it hurt my dog. My relationship with my adoptive dad was already lost. I was already heated and fed up with the abusive behaviors. As he began yanking on my dog, who was upset and hurt, I tried to gain my power back and take the leash away, but things got out of control. My adoptive dad refused to let go of the leash which left me with no choice but to put up a fight to get the leash out of his hands. Boiling inside, I kicked him. Everything happened so fast. I was on the ground and my adoptive dad was pulling my hair. Powerless, I tried getting him off me but couldn't, so I bit him. No way to escape, Sparky was barking because of the chaos that was taking place. Finally, someone came out to see what was going on.

When my adoptive mom came out and asked what was going on, I told her. I felt so boiled up on the inside that I changed my mind about going on the trip with them. I refused to go, took Sparky inside with me and made my way to my room. As protective as I was over my sister, I also was protective of my animals. Still upset, I started kicking my closet door. Adoptive mom was only concerned about going to California to visit her son. She didn't bother to ask how I was holding up even as I was in tears in front of her.

Once again, she ignored the situation. I boiled over in anger, still in my room, as they finished packing up. After they finish packing up the rest of the luggage my adoptive mom made her way into my room and says "let's go." I continued to rebel and she tried picking me up forcefully. Even as I was being dragged by the arm I continued to put up a fight and ended up on the kitchen floor. Adoptive mom sat on top of me. I was on my stomach being re-strained. I screamed and cried for her to get off of me, but she wouldn't. I fought her back. My adoptive dad came into the kitchen and said," Don't touch my wife" as I was still face down on the kitchen floor. I wrestled her again trying to escape but was defeated. My adoptive dad, positioned at the ends of my feet, took off his belt and tried to wrap the belt around my ankles but something stopped him from doing that.

I could see him positioned where he was because although I could barely tilt my head. I saw him there taking his belt off. Terrified, I called out to my younger sister who was watching all of this, asking her to call someone. She didn't call anyone. She was frozen there. I had to come to terms with my defeat. I said "fine, I will go," so the torment would stop. I got up off the floor in anger. We all made our way to the vehicle and take off.

The best way I could cope in that very moment was by choosing to purposely sit in the back. I was crying so hard that I began to cough and gag, and I spat in the cup holder. I remember making a stop at a market to buy snacks. I was not a priority, even after everything that had happened. There was never an apology and I went on that trip feeling miserable. I did not feel any sort of remorse and I sat in silence the whole trip. In pain. Hours passed and we arrived at the apartment. My adoptive mom must have informed my oldest brother about me kicking them. I recall him making a remark about me kicking his parents. I don't believe he was given the full story so I just brushed off my deep agony and tried making the best of the visit.

We left the apartment and explored a museum, walked downtown, and ate. I binge shopped whenever I felt an overwhelming stress come over me. I found some clothing items I liked and my adoptive dad purchased them. Money appeared to be the solution to solving issues. Facing the white elephant in the room was impossible. No one wanted to confront the event that happened prior to the visit. If I was going to be there feeling hurt, I had to play it off like it didn't happen. It was unjust.

We visited with my adoptive brother's family for a week, played games, and hung out with my nephews. When the trip came to an end, we went back into that toxic and abusive house with abusive parents, and I kept myself isolated. I was still in their custody. I questioned myself daily. "Why was I adopted?" I didn't hesitate to question them either.

Once, on a game day for my Korean sister, at Salem Keizer Softball field, Leslie Middle School, I was with an adoptive mom, dad and sister in-law and we watched her play. It wasn't long before I had to attend my softball practice up in West Salem. My adoptive dad dropped me off and left to go back to her game while I was at practice. Practice lasted about two hours and when the time came for my adoptive dad to pick me up I was having a conversation with my team. He called for me and practiced being over, I took my equipment and began making my way to him. As we started making our way to the van, I heard my name being called by my coach. I stopped because we hadn't gotten too far from the field.

Not knowing what my name was being called for, I ran over to see what my coach wanted. I was on the field for around five minutes checking in with my coaches and teammates. I was unsure what to expect when the coach called me back.

The coach wanted to talk to me about the game we had played over the weekend. That was it. My adoptive dad yelled my name because he was getting impatient and was upset. He began walking back towards the field and shouted out, "What makes you think you're important?" He exclaimed it loud enough that my entire team and coaches heard him. I walked away humiliated after hearing those words. I wanted to break down in tears but had to contain myself.

Those words stabbed my heart as we were making our way to the parking lot. The only thing I was able to do was avoid him. I avoided him by sitting in the very back of the van as I wept in silence with tears running down my face. This outburst was all because he wanted to go back to my sister's game so he wouldn't miss out on the last few innings. When we arrived and made our way down to the field, I walked behind hurt and in tears. We got to the game field and I remember making an attempt to talk to my adoptive mom about what happened, but she said she "couldn't."

I ended up taking a lap around the track field before the game was over in order to help me calm down. I went home that night and cried myself to sleep. My adoptive mom didn't show any interest in asking if I was okay or hearing what had transpired. The best thing I could do was continue to suppress all of the hurt and pain while living in that environment.

Abuse in public and home was unbearable. There were moments when we were out in a public setting and I wasn't obedient. I remember being yanked by my arm if obedience wasn't in order. My reactions to the abuse were punished. It was as though I wasn't allowed permission to feel hurt, let alone to express emotion. Sometimes pinching was involved as a measure of control or our wrists were aggressively tugged.

There was a lot of abuse going on behind the scenes that no one knew about. One time I had a load of laundry in the wash throughout the night. The next morning I went downstairs to switch over my laundry to the dryer but came in to find out that my laundry had been taken out of the wash. I found my wet laundry dumped in the garage.

Seeing my laundry wet and on the ground upset me. I found out that my adoptive mom was upset about the washing machine overflowing. The garage was soaked because it had leaked. This was not the first time that the washer had leaked but this time it seemed to be a major deal because I had washed my clothes. We had an argument regarding the washer and my clothes being thrown on the ground. It ticked me off because when I tried putting my clothes from the garage floor into the dryer that night, she wouldn't let me. The argument went on for a while, till I'd enough. I was so infuriated that I went upstairs, grabbed a blanket and my dog, and slept in a family friend's boat that we keep in the barn. The night was cold and rainy. I wasn't the most comfortable but made it through the night. I Spent a lot of my time that day with my dog. I left my stuff in the barn because I wasn't ready to come back inside, but I was still very upset. That day I spent my time outside playing with my dog in the field.

Another night followed and I was ready to come back inside after that night but adoptive mom wouldn't let me in. All because I made the choice to escape that night into the barn. I was left with no other choice but to spend another night in the barn with my dog. I survived the night and came back inside early morning and went to my bedroom and remained there the rest of the day just sleeping. A lot of the emotions, pain and hurt were shed through tears.

The Unexpected

There was a time where I was forced to stay up late to complete a math homework assignment that I just could not understand. I was told that I wasn't allowed to go to bed till I got the homework done. I sat at the table for hours just trying to figure out the math problems but could not. I was working on homework till midnight when everyone else was asleep. My adoptive mom slept on the couch a lot. Even so, I eventually got so tired that I couldn't sit at the table any longer. Eventually, I got up from the table and went to sleep.

I woke up the next morning and continued with the problem. My adoptive mom tried explaining the problem to me but It wasn't clicking in my head because I didn't understanding how to work out what was being asked of me. It got to the point where my adoptive mom grew upset, yelling, and losing her patience. Adoptive mem grew so upset that she tipped over the chair I was sitting in. I ended up falling backwards. It was a rapid fall. Unexpected. While some of the abuse and neglect was going on in the house, I remember my sister being forced to live in the basement with very few of her belongings. She was in a small corner where dolls and a shelf full of movies were set up. In the tiny space she had, there was a bedding sheet hung-up for her privacy. I'm telling you, seeing my sister living in that tiny corner area brought negative emotions to me. My sister being forced out of the bedroom she was in and made to live downstairs with very little privacy was wrong. She was already going through her own issues with our abusive parents. My adoptive dad mentally abused her by saying she was "stupid" or "retarded." My sister, already suffering from the mental, emotional, and physical abuse that was going on, tried killing herself during the time she was staying in her room. When she broke the glass window and attempted suicide things got out of control. She wrote very dark phrases on her wall, which brought fear to my parents. Writing on the wall lead my adoptive dad to believe that my sister was a monster, a demon possessed. Fear instilled in that idea she might try and hurt the family. Her window was broken and the brothers left in the house at the time were the ones who took protective measures around the window. She wouldn't be able to get out, bring harm to herself, or escape. The window was plastered with built-in boards on the inside, secured across each other, in an X shaped figure.

As this was going on, both adoptive parents decided that my sister staying in the house wasn't a good idea because the writings on the wall threatened family lives. Sometime that morning the cops were called and involved in the situation. I remember the cops chaining my sister's hands and taking her away from the home. They thought she was deeply disturbed and troubled so that was their solution to this problem.

After some time, my sister was taken to a family friend. This family friend took her in and nurtured her for weeks and months. Every now and then Sarah visited with the family, but the visits weren't always pleasant. On days that the family friend wasn't able to watch my sister, she stayed with the family. Even then, the matters within the abusive and toxic environment didn't help anything or anyone. If the stay with my sister wasn't convenient during the day, she spent with the family, or our adoptive mom would bring her to another family friend. This gave my adoptive mom a break from having to deal with my sister. It became a recognizable pattern.

During my twin sister's adolescent years with the family, she was struggling. Our adoptive mom received a call from a local Walmart and was informed that Sarah had been caught stealing make-up. This is the period when my sister started rebelling. When she rebelled, she was punished on family outings.

When the family went out to restaurants my sister would be stopped from ordering food. She would sit at the table and watch everyone else, her brothers and sisters, eat. I recall moments of both parents forcing our siblings to withhold any form of interaction or engagement with her if she was disobedient or didn't give them the apology that they were wanting out of her. Throughout my adolescent years, I also experienced similar punishment. If I misbehaved, I was forbidden from enjoying family outings and going out to restaurants. If I was allowed to go, I was not able to order food. Just like my sister, my parents would not allow my siblings to speak to me if my attitude didn't change, I was disobedient, or didn't give them an apology for not obeying them.

My sister had long gone out of the house when my problems with the family started but we went through similar experiences. The abuse never seemed to stop. Whether it was emotional, mental, or physical, I have memories of many consequences.

One experience happened after my phone was taken away. I was interrogated by both adoptive parents and was accused of accessing my phone when it was impossible for me to do so. I say impossible because they had grounded me from it. I had been asked if I had used my phone and I answered "no" which was the truth, but they continued to believe that I was lying. I was flustered at being accused of using the phone when I possibly could not have. An argument ensued about me possibly using the phone which led to a heated argument that night. We had a yelling match, and I argued back with them, convincing them if they ever thought of my phone being hacked. They were so adamant about it being me that there was no winning. They didn't even try to hear me out. I became used to not being believed or listened to, so this was nothing new to me. I was the child, and they were the parents.

A lot was said that night, but as I sat in the rocking chair, my adoptive mom decided to get up in my face. I could already see the anger in her eyes as she tried to get the truth out of me. I had already told the truth but it didn't matter. I hated the fact that she was up in my face, once again, and tried pushing her away. She had a habit of doing this to me and my sister, pushing our boundaries when we did not want to be physical.

I tried pushing her away from me but she just would not back off, but this didn't come as a surprise to me because that was her way of handling things with us. The struggle continued for a few more minutes and I felt that she left me with no choice but to be physical. I used my upper body strength to get her away from me and managed to escape from where I was sitting. Distanced to a different chair, I was boiling inside with rage. I made a remark that I recall upset my adoptive dad which he did not take lightly. He walked across from the other side of the family room and slapped me across the face. I was so sick and tired of the nonsense and without hesitation I walked out into the pitch dark. I left out of anger, in tears at the thought of existing in the presence of my so called "family."

Aa I walked, I went through a list of people who I could escape to. The individual that came to my mind was my grandma. She was closer than any of the church members that were going through my head, so I chose to go that direction. My youngest brother went chasing after me when I didn't want him to, but he did. The walk was long but I was in a mindset and my brother wasn't going to stop me. Especially when I was ticked off. I made it all the way past Creekside golf course down Sunnyside road. We had crossed the road of our grandma's and my adoptive brother that his mom, letting her know where we were and she came and picked us up. On the car ride home I remained silent. When we arrived home, I went straight to my room with no further interaction with both adoptive parents. I went to bed, sad, hurt, and angry. The next morning, my adoptive parents found out that it had not been me that logged into my Facebook or Instagram account. I overheard them talking about it. The worst of it all was never receiving any form of apology from them even though I apologized constantly.

I came to accept life with my adoptive family. I knew that the abuse was wrong and so did my adoptive brothers and sisters but it didn't matter. The expression "White Elephant in the Room" greatly suited this family. I felt suffocated and I learned to suppress a lot of my emotions. I went about living my life in a great deal of pain. Christian friends and family saw me as a happy girl when in reality my life was a living hell.

I learned to put on a front in public. I taught myself to play different roles of character and personality throughout day to day living even when people weren't aware. Sometimes I couldn't avoid crying in public and I was largely ignored. Some people tried to engage in conversation about things that didn't seem right with either me or my sister. Most often, people would be too scared to ask what was wrong. It didn't help matters that our adoptive parents kept us in their sight. We had no chance to explain. Besides, If I decided to leave home for good where would I go and who could I trust? During the chaos, I found it very difficult for myself to retain educational information in such a toxic and broken home. Education became difficult, especially when a lot of my energy, time and focus was spent on protecting myself. Homeschooled for nine years of my life made learning an even greater challenge. How is a child expected to learn when abuse is going on?

When I started high school, I was given the decision to either attend public school or to continue being homeschooled through this Christian online Academy called "Abeka". Abeka was a Christian homeschool education that taught reading, math, creative writing, spelling, grammar, vocabulary, history and science. When given a choice, I chose to attend public school. I felt as though I was missing out on experiences of being a teen. I was curious about what the environment, setting, and experience would be like attending a school that was outside of homeschooling, and I wanted to try it out. I was excited at first because I would have a chance to be around other kids my age. Not only this, but I wanted this time to be able to make connections beyond the limited experience I had around other homeschool kids. I was full of energy, outgoing, friendly, and sociable so it only made sense to me to try something out of my comfort zone. A final decision about school had not been made before a situation had developed. I recall being in my room, sitting on the top bunk of my bed, hearing my adoptive mom and dad argue about whether they should send me to public school. Their voices were loud enough that it made it impossible not to hear what they were fighting about.

My adoptive dad wasn't pleased with the idea of sending me to public school. He didn't want me to learn alone, and he didn't believe that I could earn good grades. He was concerned about spending money on an education that he wasn't confident about. The assumption was that I could not be educated because I wasn't willing to learn. This wasn't the case.

If only they had taken a step back to examine, or reflect on, what was going on in the home they may not have had this argument. Unfortunately, they were ignorant to the toxic environment my sister and I were in due to their abuse of us. To adoptive dad, I was already a lost cause and he believed I would be capable of succeeding if the bar was set very low. With his four sons academically advanced as well as my Korean sister I was left feeling that I would be an embarrassment to the family. I felt more alone, discouraged, and unsupported than ever.

I desired to go to school like other kids my age and I wanted to engage in the game of Softball. My adoptive parents eventually came to an agreement and let me attend school. This gave me something to look forward to, even though my self-esteem was impacted because of their lack of faith in me, their lack of encouragement and support.

Unstoppable, I committed to attending my first year so that I could experience an adventure of something beyond the bubble I was living in. When the time came, I did well. My best effort, energy, and hard work were put into succeeding even though I was struggling academically at home. I wasn't a straight A student but I didn't consider myself to be a failure either. I passed my classes and received the grades I needed to be able to participate in Softball.

This made me happy, and I kept up with my grades. I continued to play throughout my Freshman and Junior year before life took a turn.

My freshman experience in a real school was not at all easy. The environment was highly populated, which I wasn't prepared for. I wasn't familiar with such a large social circle, and it brought with it a high level of anxiety. I felt self-conscious about being smart enough which created worry about how my success would compare to that of my peers. Education was already a huge challenge, even in Liberia. My sister and I missed out on important schooling due to poverty making it unaffordable to gain proper education. Coming to a strange world, I had to do a lot of catching up for missed opportunities in academic success.

Dear Younger Self,
Being homeschooled didn't help you out. Back then, you didn't grasp what it meant to be properly educated and informed about the world but you will. You will be aware of more than what was taught to you. At twenty-one years old you will remember what you learned through observation and listening.

With hard work in school, I was able to maintain grades that allowed me to play the game of Softball. The years I spent playing, traveling, and engaging in tournaments created in me a new and profound identity. Softball gave me meaning, something that helped me escape from the reality I was living in and always had to go back to. Sprague was where my love for Softball started and where I met new friends and families. I started catching for a teammate of mine during freshman year at Sprague and played little league with my sister.

Over the years, I got acquainted with my teammate's family and they soon became my sports family who I traveled with to a lot of my Softball tournaments, games, and practices. We would have early morning wake up tournament games and they would take me to those games and to many practices. I was going through so much at home that there were times when I felt rejected. Being handed off to different people is what my life came to. When I started playing at Sprague, my adoptive parents were more attentive, and they showed up more at my games than ever. They were often present during Basketball games because it didn't require out of state travel. The games at Sprague were local, so it was an easy drive. Basketball was local and played in churches throughout Salem, so it never conflicted with their schedule. As the years went on, they gradually became less involved in my life when it came to competitions due to out-of-range locations. Some games weren't too far out of Oregon, so my adoptive parents accommodated their schedule to see my games. There were some sacrifices made after Sunday church to come to watch me play. When my siblings and parents were able to attend more local games it felt like I had a family, like I belonged somewhere. Life wasn't this simple for me though.

I had so much going on and softball was the only thing that kept my mind off my life at home. It was great having Softball as a fun interest and hobby. On hard days I would lose. I gave my all to games when I was in a good head space. I held my head high through some of those tough times while playing and I didn't talk about my personal life with teammates. Softball was my identity. until the age of fifteen. My Softball life came to an end and I realized I didn't have Softball to escape to anymore. I had to face the music with the upcoming challenges that were ahead.

Beginning of A New Journey

Dealing with all the trauma and abuse of my life put me in a place where at age fifteen I got in trouble with the law. It happened one night when my sister's friend spent the night, and the events of the night led to me going into the Marion County Juvenile Court System. The offense was the leading factor that forced counseling into the hands of my parents. It wasn't till this event that my counseling work started, long after it should have. I had never been given the proper counseling and I had needed appropriate tools to manage the stressors of my life. The counseling I received was through religion. I was sent to the pastor at Salem First Baptist where family therapy began. Let me tell you, this didn't help matters with life at home. It was a great tool for me to vent frustrations, yes. But it didn't give me a chance to really share the deep wounds I was carrying from years of emotional damage, abuse, and trauma that played a role in my day-to-day life. Family therapy sessions didn't help my adoptive parents change their ways.

They remained stuck in ignorance and denial. I did not believe in their parenting style because it created more problems than it fixed. It didn't help matters when they didn't want help with parenting because they believed their way was right. My adoptive dad didn't want other people interfering with his parenting. Being in the family sessions kept me silent because my adoptive parents would be present in most of those sessions. I left sessions with nothing major being resolved and went back into the same toxic and abusive environment.

The constant feeling of rejection, neglect and abuse pushed me over the edge. I felt rejected when I was left behind from family outings, some family vacation trips and camping trips. Being rejected hurt but I always got through the painful times. Sometimes I was dropped off to stay with family friends. In fact, a lot of my time was spent with family, friends or grandparents. This made my life feel out of place, but it was better than being home. There were moments when I was happy because I had to be. My choices were very limited, so I saved my sanity by suppressing irritable emotions and frustrations, acting happy when inside when I was in a lot of pain. I didn't let people see that side of me. I maintained the representation and expectation that people had of me whenever I could throughout daily challenges and triumphs. I had long gone into depression but kept up the act by smiling through the pain and hurt.

Abuse led to abuse and without the necessary guidance and help I should have received from my adoptive parents it led to the situation where I abused my sister's friend sexually. After that night there was no turning back. I faced he consequences of my actions which I was not prepared for, but something had to happen, and it did. I didn't sleep much that night and woke up the following morning worried and fearful. I had to pay my dues and that's exactly what led to the journey I'm on today. More will be shared as I continue writing my story.

The only picture I have with my family from
Liberia.

The girl who kept hope alive
when hope felt lost.

My name is Konah and I am 24 years old. I am a girl who
kept hope alive when hope felt lost. I am an adoptee from Liberia, Africa. Was adopted at the age of six with my twin sister and
brought here to America, eighteen years ago now. Raised in poverty, left to fend for myself without the help, protection, or support of
my birth parents. As a six-year-old girl coming out of poverty and
war, life in America has been a challenge. I am a survivor of war,
adoption trauma, poverty, and generational abuse. Rising above my
personal history by seeking opportunities for personal success and
growth is my opportunity. With the losses I have endured throughout my life from a young age has strengthened my personal growth
and development. After years of working through challenging mental health issues, I have returned to Lane Community College more
motivated than ever to earn my ASS degree in Social Work. For

this reason, I am currently working on pursuing higher education through Social work / Human Services. I envision a future where I am working in the Department of Human Services through adoption, providing housing services in the community to children from a variety of backgrounds and with varying needs who are awaiting a family to take them in with the extra guidance and support from a loving family that has their best interest at heart, where I can share my experiences of hardships, so that others can find hope when there seems to be none. My own adoption is a self-reflection of how lonely my adoption journey has been. The process in which I am still standing before you today has not been easy.

Publisher's Note

Daxson publishing was created to help marginalized artists publish their work, so the world can hear their voice. The vision for this publishing house is to help people get their work out there, and not have them struggle finding their way through the publishing process. Everyone's voice deserves to be heard, and we are here to help. If you are interested in submitting a manuscript, email daxsonpublishing@gmail.com.